CULTURE in the Kitchen

FOODS OF India

By Mary Molly Shea

Gareth Stevens
Publishing

Please visit our website, www.garethstevens.com. For a free color catalog of all our high-quality books, call toll free 1-800-542-2595 or fax 1-877-542-2596.

Library of Congress Cataloging-in-Publication Data

Shea, Mary Molly.
Foods of India / Mary Molly Shea.
    p. cm. — (Culture in the kitchen)
Includes index.
ISBN 978-1-4339-5708-6 (pbk.)
ISBN 978-1-4339-5709-3 (6-pack)
ISBN 978-1-4339-5706-2 (library binding)
1. India—Social life and customs—Juvenile literature. 2. Cooking, India—Juvenile literature. 3. Food habits—India—Juvenile literature. I. Title.
TX724.5.I4S424 2011
641.5954—dc22

                                2010048165

First Edition

Published in 2012 by
Gareth Stevens Publishing
111 East 14th Street, Suite 349
New York, NY 10003

Copyright © 2012 Gareth Stevens Publishing

Designer: Daniel Hosek
Editor: Therese Shea

Photo credits: Cover and all images Shutterstock.com.

Printed in the United States of America

CPSIA compliance information: Batch #CS11GS: For further information contact Gareth Stevens, New York, New York at 1-800-542-2595.

Contents

Words in the glossary appear in **bold** type the first time they are used in the text.

The Country of India

India is a country in south Asia. It's second only to China in population. India's people are among the most **diverse** on Earth. They speak different languages, honor different **religions**, and follow different ways of life. With so many differences, it's no wonder that Indian food is diverse as well.

Indian restaurants have become popular in the United States in recent years. People from all backgrounds count Indian dishes as some of their favorites. Have you ever eaten Indian food? After reading more, you'll want to!

Asia

India

India is a
country rich
in history.
Visitors today
can see
palaces and
forts built
hundreds of
years ago.

5

The Grains of India

Most Indians eat two or three meals a day. The basic Indian meal is made up of several parts. The biggest part contains grains. In eastern and southern India, people eat rice. In other **regions** of India, people eat bread. In the north and northwest, wheat is harvested, ground, and made into a flat bread called chapati.

A grain called pearl millet, or bajra, is a main crop in western India. It, too, can be made into bread.

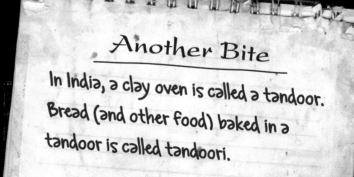

bajra

Another Bite

In India, a clay oven is called a tandoor. Bread (and other food) baked in a tandoor is called tandoori.

6

Chapati bakes quickly on a metal plate over a hot fire.

The Rest of the Meal

In an Indian meal, beans, peas, or **lentils** are usually eaten with bread or rice. They are cooked into dishes called dals. For those who can afford

dal

it, yogurt may be eaten as well. If available, vegetables, fruits, and milk are added to the meal.

Most Indians don't eat meat often. Meat dishes are saved for special celebrations. Fish, however, is commonly eaten in places near the coast.

Many people in India are poor, so meals are often small.

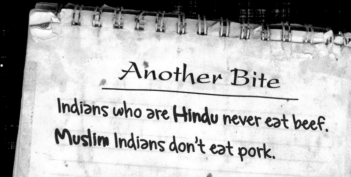

Another Bite

Indians who are Hindu never eat beef. Muslim Indians don't eat pork.

Indian farmers bring their fruits and vegetables to sell in city markets.

9

Spices

Much of Indian food wouldn't have a lot of **flavor** without some extra **ingredients**. India is known for its spices. However, the spices aren't only added for flavor. Many are also thought to make people healthier.

In India, a mix of spices is called a masala. The mix is added to liquids such as water, cream, or vinegar and blended into a sauce. The ingredients in a masala differ from region to region. In other countries, both the spice mix and the spicy dish may be called curry.

cardamom

Another Bite

In India, pepper is believed to aid stomach illnesses. A spice called cardamom is said to provide relief from fever and headaches.

spices

◀ The basic curry or masala mix includes turmeric (which gives it a yellow color), cumin, coriander, and red pepper.

11

Northern India has hot summers and cold winters. Fruits and vegetables grow well in many areas. People in this region eat chapatis as their main food. Bread called naan is also served. Some Indian breads are flat, like chapatis, while others use yeast to rise, like naan. Samosas are bread "pockets" with meat or vegetables inside.

The masalas of the north are rarely spicy. Ingredients include cardamom, cinnamon, clove, and black pepper. Dried fruits, nuts, and dairy products are also added to northern Indian dishes.

Punjabi dish

Another Bite

The state of Punjab is in northern India. Most Indian restaurants in western countries such as the United States serve Punjabi dishes.

The northern Indian dish shown at the bottom of the page is called saag. It is made with leafy green vegetables. Naan is shown at the top of the page.

Foods of Western India

Some parts of western India are covered by desert. These areas don't often have fresh fruits and vegetables available. People of western India **pickle** the fruits and vegetables on hand to make them last longer. These pickled foods are called achar.

To the south of the desert is the city of Mumbai, where fishermen bring in many kinds of seafood. Even further south, vindaloo is a popular spicy dish consisting of meat, vinegar, and chili peppers.

mango achar

The red color of chicken vindaloo hints at the dish's very spicy flavor.

Foods of Southern India

All states of southern India are close to the sea. In this region, cooks use fish and coconut in their dishes. In the center of the southern region, a spice called tamarind creates an almost sour taste in dishes. To the west are found foods such as lamb stew and steamed rice cakes called idlis.

Also common are dosas, which are pancakes made of rice and lentils that are stuffed with vegetables. Dosas may be served with chutney, which is a sweet and spicy mix of fruits.

Another Bite

Similar Indian dishes may have different names. Hundreds of languages are spoken in India. About three-fifths of the people speak Hindi.

These dosas are served with aloo masala, which is a spicy potato dish.

Foods of Eastern India

In eastern India, heavy rains help huge crops of rice, fruits, and vegetables grow each year. Near the Bay of Bengal, it's common to mix rice and fish. The hilsa fish is sometimes wrapped in pumpkin leaves before it's cooked. Further from the coast, pork is a popular meat. Bamboo shoots are sometimes used in preparing food as well.

This region is well known for its sweets. Sandesh is made from sugar, pistachio nuts, and cheese called paneer. Rosogollas are treats made of milk, flour, sugar, and rose water.

Another Bite

The village of Cherrapunji in eastern India receives about 450 inches (1,143 cm) of rain each year!

Sandesh and other desserts are an important part of Bengali celebrations.

Drinks of India

Tea is the common drink in northern and eastern India, while coffee is more common in southern India. An Indian drink called chai mixes black tea, cream, and the spices of cinnamon, cardamom, clove, and ginger. Together, these make a creamy, sweet drink that has become popular worldwide.

Lassi is a sugary yogurt drink, and Indian soda mixes a fizzy drink with lime and salt. Fruit juices (mango, guava, and other fruits) and coconut milk are also popular.

lassi

Recipe:
Chapati

(requires the help of an adult)

Ingredients:

1 1/2 cups whole-wheat flour

1/2 cup all-purpose flour

1 teaspoon salt

1 tablespoon vegetable oil

1/2 to 3/4 cup warm water

melted butter (optional)

Directions:

1. In a bowl, mix flours, salt, oil, and enough water to form a soft **dough**. **Knead** the dough ten times, then cover for 1 hour.

2. Form 10 balls from the dough. On a lightly floured surface, roll out the balls into 6-inch (15-cm) circles.

3. Heat an ungreased pan over medium-high heat. Lay the circles on the hot pan one at a time. Cook until the dough starts to puff. Then turn and cook until golden brown spots form.

4. Remove chapatis, place on a kitchen towel, and brush with melted butter if you wish.

Glossary

diverse: differing from each other

dough: a mix of flour and water

flavor: a feature of a food or drink that gives it a special taste

Hindu: a follower of a major religion of south Asia

ingredient: a part of a mixture

knead: to work with dough until it's smooth

lentil: a seed that comes from a plant in the pea family and can be eaten

Muslim: a follower of the religion of Islam

pickle: to add a mixture of vinegar or salt to a food to make it last longer

region: a large area of land that has features that make it different from nearby areas of land

religion: a belief in and way of honoring a god or gods

For More Information

Books

Ganeri, Anita. *India*. Minneapolis, MN: Clara House Books, 2010.

Goodman, Polly. *Food in India*. New York, NY: PowerKids Press, 2008.

Websites

Authentic Indian Food Recipes from India

indianrecipe.org

Watch video recipes, and find out about many famous meals of India.

Indian Food

www.historyforkids.org/learn/india/food/

Read about the history of Indian food, and see a video of an Indian boy making bread.

Index